POP CULTURE BIOS

LITTLE MIX

SINGERS WITH X-TRA SUCCESS

HEATHER E. SCHWARTZ

Lerner Publications Company
MINNEAPOLIS

Lerner Publications Company
A division of Lerner Publishing Group, Inc.
241 First Avenue North
Minneapolis, MN 55401 USA

For reading levels and more information, look up this title at
www.lernerbooks.com.

Library of Congress Cataloging-in-Publication Data

Schwartz, Heather E., author.
      Little Mix : singers with x-tra success / by Heather E.
Schwartz.
        pages   cm. — (Pop culture bios)
      Includes index.
      ISBN 978–1–4677–3668–8 (lib. bdg. : alk. paper)
      ISBN 978–1–4677–4732–5 (eBook)
      1. Little Mix (Musical group)—Juvenile literature. 2. Rock
musicians—England—Biography—Juvenile literature. 3. Women
rock musicians—England—Biography—Juvenile literature.
I. Title.
ML421.L594S39 2015
782.421649092'2—dc23 [B]   2013046314

Manufactured in the United States of America
1 – PC – 7/15/14

INTRODUCTION

Jade Thirlwall

Little Mix members (LEFT TO RIGHT)
Perrie Edwards, Jade Thirlwall, Jesy
Nelson, and Leigh-Anne Pinnock

Perrie Edwards, Leigh-Anne Pinnock, Jesy Nelson, and Jade Thirlwall entered John F. Kennedy International Airport in New York City. A pumped-up crowd waved and called out to them. Fans offered balloons and snapped pics. The crowd was psyched to see their favorite British band, Little Mix, on US soil.

Little Mix poses in Los Angeles, California, at the *Teen Vogue* back-to-school kickoff party.

The band members worked their way through the crowd. They smiled, chatted, and signed autographs graciously. Yet they were surprised to learn how popular they were in the United States. As they traveled the country, they grew even more surprised. Fans were tracking the band and waiting for the girls at each destination. One devoted fan even chased their tour bus on foot—for two hundred blocks!

In 2011, two years earlier, the members of Little Mix had been living normal lives in Britain. Back then, they didn't know one another. They weren't famous at all. But a lot had changed. Their experience in the United States was proof of just how far they'd come. Little Mix was an international act now. The band members were real pop stars.

They were excited and overwhelmed. They were also really, really happy. Their ordinary lives had morphed into a dream come true.

Little Mix performing at the Teen Vogue back-to-school kickoff party

Perrie Edwards

Jade Thirlwall

CHAPTER ONE

FOUR GIRLS, ONE DREAM

Jesy Nelson

Leigh-Anne Pinnock

In 2011, four British girls had the same dream. They all wanted to be singers. So why not audition for a reality show that could help them reach that goal?

The girls had never met. They didn't know anything about one another's hopes and dreams. But they all decided—separately—to audition for the eighth season of *The X Factor* in the United Kingdom. Who were the girls before they tried out for the show?

AUDITION =
to perform in hopes of earning a part

Perrie Edwards

Perrie's parents were singers. So becoming one herself didn't seem *too* out there. Still, she was scared to try. But then her mom offered her an iPhone if she'd give it a shot.

Jesy Nelson

Jesy liked singing and dancing, but she was shy about performing—even for her family. While working as a bartender, she got the courage to go for it on *The X Factor*.

Both Perrie and Jade are from South Shields, a coastal town in northeastern England.

Jesy grew up in Romford, a suburban town of London, England.

Leigh-Anne Pinnock

After high school, Leigh-Anne hoped to make it in music. Meanwhile, before *The X Factor*, she earned her keep as a Pizza Hut server.

Jade Thirlwall

As a child, Jade was so serious about a showbiz career that she attended a performing school. Of the four, she was the only one who'd been on *The X Factor* before—twice.

Leigh-Anne grew up in High Wycombe, a town in southeastern England.

LITTLE MIX BIRTHDAYS

PERRIE: July 10, 1993
LEIGH-ANNE: October 4, 1991
JESY: June 14, 1991
JADE: December 26, 1992

Solo Acts

As solo artists, the girls impressed *The X Factor* judges during their auditions…mostly. Jade crooned "I Want to Hold Your Hand" by the Beatles. Leigh-Anne showed off tons of attitude performing Rihanna's "Only Girl (in the World)."

The girls leave an X Factor practice.

Singing "You Oughta Know" by Alanis Morissette, Perrie was sure she'd be rejected. "I was absolutely petrified. **I didn't tell anybody I was going in for the audition,"** she said later. Perrie did much better than she'd expected. Judge Kelly Rowland called her voice "crazy" (in a good way!).

Perrie's unique voice got her through to the next round.

The *X Factor* judges came to the 2011 show with experience in the music business. They were as follows:

GARY BARLOW: British singer/songwriter

TULISA CONTOSTAVLOS: British singer/songwriter

KELLY ROWLAND: American singer/songwriter

LOUIS WALSH: Irish entertainment promoter and manager

Jesy, however, didn't fare so well. She belted out "Bust Your Windows" by Jazmine Sullivan. Judge Gary Barlow panned her performance and called her "generic."

"He absolutely hated me," Jesy later recalled. "I remember thinking, 'I want the crowd to swallow me up.' It was just so embarrassing."

Even so, she wasn't dismissed. And all four singers made it to the show's next level: boot camp.

Teaming Up

In boot camp, the judges put them in two separate girl bands. Perrie and Jesy were in Faux Pas. Jade and Leigh-Anne were in Orion. But the bands weren't working out. All four singers were about to be booted. Thankfully, the judges gave them the chance to perform together. It was their last chance to stay in the competition. The girls called their new band Rhythmix. In just twenty-four hours, they prepared to prove to the judges they were in it to win it. Their performance got them out of boot camp. Next, they'd have a shot at performing in live shows.

MUSICAL ICONS INSPIRATIONS

The members of Little Mix are inspired by their fav musicians.
Perrie: Steve Perry of Journey
Jesy: Missy Elliott
Leigh-Anne: Rihanna, Justin Bieber, Aaliyah
Jade: Amy Winehouse

CHAPTER TWO

LITTLE MIX IS BORN

Little Mix with their X Factor mentor, Tulisa Contostavlos (MIDDLE)

During the next phase of the competition—the live shows—the girl group had to outperform the other finalists. But the group also faced an unexpected challenge. A British charity organization called Rhythmix didn't like sharing the name with the band. The charity wanted the band to change its name. The singers had no problem making a quick switch. After some brainstorming with their *X Factor* mentor, Tulisa, Little Mix was born.

The girls developed an unbreakable bond during the show.

BIG-SCREEN FAVS

Even popular performers need a break sometimes. The Little Mix members have their all-time favorite flicks they veg out with.

Perrie: *The Notebook*

Jesy: *Taken*

Leigh-Anne: *Titanic* and *Jason's Lyric*

Jade: *P.S. I Love You* and *Seven Pounds*

Life in the Spotlight

Little Mix was hugely famous even before the competition ended. Millions of *X Factor* viewers already loved them for their incredible voices, sweet attitudes, and style the singers called "urban geek."

Fame definitely had its advantages. The girls got to put their performing talents to the test. They wore ever-more-amazing outfits and rubbed elbows with superstars.

FASHION INSPIRATIONS

The members of Little Mix love looking creative. They draw inspiration from other fashion icons. Perrie looks to Kelly Kapowski of the '90s TV show *Saved by the Bell* for fashion tips. Leigh-Anne is a fan of Will Smith's style from another '90s show, *The Fresh Prince of Bel-Air*. Jade takes her ideas from rapper Labrinth. And Jesy likes Gwen Stefani's signature style.

Perrie even started dating cutie Zayn Malik of the band One Direction. The two met when the band performed on *The X-Factor*.

But fame had a downside too. The media reported on every aspect of Perrie and Zayn's relationship, including rumors that Zayn was cheating. Haters targeted Jesy too. She was cyberbullied by anti-fans about her weight. Their nasty comments brought her to tears. But the other girls helped her through it. They may have met only weeks before, but their bond as bandmates was already rock solid.

Zayn Malik performing with his band One Direction

Fans loved Little Mix's take on "Cannonball" when they performed on *The X Factor*. It was a perfect pick for the band's first single.

And the Winner Is...

By mid-December 2011, the competition was down to three: Little Mix and soloists Marcus Collins and Amelia Lily.

Little Mix sang Damien Rice's "Cannonball" during the final. The crowd and the judges couldn't contain their excitement. **"Girls, you've done everything you were told. You deserve the votes,"** Louis Walsh said. "Vote for Little Mix!"

SINGLE = a song released separately from a full album, often for radio play

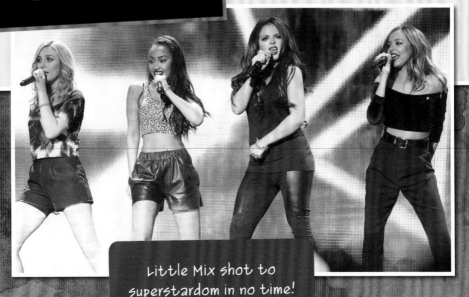

Little Mix shot to superstardom in no time!

With the judges on their side, the girls' fate was up to the public vote. Waiting onstage to learn who'd won, the girls held hands. Their faces were tense. At last, they heard their name. Little Mix had won! The crowd erupted with cheers and applause. The singers jumped up and down. They screamed and hugged one another.

They were so overwhelmed that they could barely speak. Leigh-Anne looked stunned. "Oh my gosh. Wow!" she said. She didn't seem able to say anything more. Jade chimed in next. **"We're just so, so grateful and thankful to everyone who voted,"** she said. Her voice was filled with emotion. She and the others wiped tears from their cheeks.

They were the first girl group to ever win on *The X Factor*. And their victory was just the beginning of an exciting future as a band.

LOYAL FANS

What do Little Mix fans call themselves? Mixers, of course! There are plenty of them too. The band's Facebook page has nearly 4 million "Likes." More than 4 million fans follow them on Twitter.

CHAPTER THREE

INTERNATIONAL SUPERSTARS

Little Mix has had their share of fans from the beginning. And sometimes they can act just plain strange. When the band performed in Australia in 2012, a fan licked their tour bus window!

Perrie, Jesy, Leigh-Anne, and Jade kicked off 2012 in high demand. In January, they sang "Don't Let Go (Love)" by En Vogue at the National Television Awards. In February, they posed stylishly on the red carpet at the Brit Awards. Later that spring, they attended the Glamour Women of the Year Awards with the likes of Jessica Alba, Sofía Vergara, and Eva Longoria.

Little Mix loves their fans and all the fun fame brings.

Little Mix poses at a signing for their book, *Little Mix: Ready to Fly*.

Little Mix even signed deals with companies that wanted to create products based on the band. Dolls and accessories were developed so fans could celebrate the band's talent and style. And by September, the band had released an autobiography the members wrote together. They told their full story in *Little Mix: Ready to Fly*.

Everyone knew them. Little Mix couldn't go anywhere without being recognized. But they told the media they had no complaints. Mainly, being famous was just plain fun.

SELLING THEIR STYLE

Little Mix is so popular that Collection cosmetics partnered with them in 2013. Together, they created makeup for fans who wanted to look just like the girls.

Workin' It Worldwide

The singers didn't love the spotlight just for the perks though. The real reason they were there: they had a passion for performing. Their debut album, *DNA*, came out in the United Kingdom in November 2012. A few months later, Little Mix released "How Ya Doin'?" as a single from the album. R & B legend Missy Elliott joined them on the track. They could hardly believe they were getting the chance to work with one of their idols.

R & B =
rhythm and blues

The band proudly poses with their first album, *DNA*.

COVERING THEIR SONG

Little Mix's first single release from *DNA* was "Wings." The song was featured on the US television shows *Glee* and *American Idol*.

In August 2013, Perrie was spotted wearing a diamond ring. She didn't waste any time letting the media in on her secret. She and Zayn were engaged!

In June 2013, the four Brits of Little Mix made big news in America. *DNA* ranked No. 4 on the *Billboard* 200 chart. The media compared the band to '90s girl group the Spice Girls—and pointed out that Little Mix had broken the Spice Girls' chart record. The four girls now had the highest-charting debut album for a British girl group in America.

That same month, Little Mix crossed the pond to perform in New York City on *Good Morning America*. By the end of 2013, they had a second album, *Salute*, ready for release. They were also set to travel the United States as an opening act for singer Demi Lovato on her Neon Lights tour in 2014.

Within two years, Little Mix went from normal girls to pop sensation. They are breaking out of Britain and taking on the world. With this kind of talent and dedication, who knows what the future will bring?

Jesy (LEFT) with Leigh-Anne (RIGHT) performing on *Good Morning America*

LITTLE MIX

PICS!

Little Mix poses at the 2012 Brit Awards.

SOURCE NOTES

13   *Little Mix's First Auditions as Soloists*, YouTube video, 2:38, posted by "RhythmixFans1,"
      December 19, 2011, http://www.youtube.com/watch?v=z4Y870NfGJw.

13   Ibid.

14   Ibid.

14   Ibid.

20   *Could This Be Little Mix's Winner's Single?—The X Factor 2011 Live Final* (Full Version),
      YouTube video, 6:32, posted by "The X Factor UK," December 11, 2011, http://www
      .youtube.com/watch?v=l3XQlYpIrQ0.

21   *And the Winner Is…—The X Factor 2011 Live Final* (Full Version), YouTube video, 2:69,
      posted by "The X Factor UK," December 11, 2011, http://www.youtube.com/watch?v
      =-fCimjFW4kA.

21   Ibid.

MORE LITTLE MIX INFO

Facebook
https://www.facebook.com/LittleMixOfficial
Join other Mixers by liking Little Mix's page and following their status updates.

Little Mix. *Little Mix: Ready to Fly*. London: HarperCollins, 2012. Read the official Little Mix
autobiography to learn all about Perrie, Leigh-Anne, Jesy, and Jade.

Little Mix—The Official Website
http://www.little-mix.com/us/home
Get the inside scoop on what the band is up to—straight from the girls.

Twitter
https://twitter.com/LittleMix
Follow the girls' tweets and see their photos on Twitter.

YouTube
https://www.youtube.com/user/littlemixVEVO
Watch Little Mix's latest videos on YouTube.

INDEX

The images in this book are used with the permission of: © Mike Marsland/WireImage/Getty Images, pgs. 2, 8 (Jesy and Perrie); © Jo Hale/Getty Images, pgs. 3 (Top), 9, 4 (Top Right); © Dave M. Benett/Getty Images, pgs. 3 (Bottom), 4 (Top Left), 8 (Leigh-Anne), 28 (Top Right), 29 (Top Right);; Steve Meddle/Rex USA, p. 4 (Bottom); © David Livingston/Getty Images, pgs. 5, 7, 28 (Top Left); © Dave J. Hogan/Getty Images, p. 6; © Mark Robert Milan/FilmMagic/Getty Images, p. 8 (Jade); © John Parfrey, p. 10 (Romford); © Ellen Van Bodegom/Flickr Open/Getty Images, p. 10 (South Shields); © Universal Images Group/SuperStock, p. 11; © Neil Mockford/FilmMagic/Getty Images, pgs. 12; 17, 18, 28 (Bottom); © Ben Prunchie/Getty Images, p. 13; © Fox Image Collection/Getty Images, p. 14; © Barcroft Media/Getty Images, p. 15; © Phillip Massey/WireImage/Getty Images, pgs. 16 (Top), 20; © Alex Moss/Film Magic/Getty Images, pgs. 16 (Bottom), 29 (Bottom); © Kevin Winter/AMA2013/Getty Images, p. 19; © Dave J. Hogan/Getty Images, p. 22; © Tony Woolliscroft//Getty Images, pgs. 22, 24; © Jun Sato/WireImage/Getty Images, p. 23; © William Parker/UK Press/Getty Images, p. 24; © Karwai Tang/WireImage/Getty Images, p. 26 (Inset); AP Photo/Ferex, p. 26; © Bennett Raglin/WireImage/Getty Images, p. 27; © Tommy Jackson/Redferns/Getty Images, p. 29 (Top Left); © Gareth Cattermole/Getty Images, p. 29 (Bottom)..

Front Cover: © Rob Ball/WireImage/Getty Images (all wearing black); © Shirlaine Forrest/Redferns/Getty Images (performing on stage).

Back Cover: © Samir Hussein/Getty Images.

Main body text set in Shannon Std Book 12/18.
Typeface provided by Monotype Typography.